COMPREHENSION NINJA WORKBOOK

AGES 7–8

ANDREW JENNINGS

BLOOMSBURY EDUCATION

LONDON   OXFORD   NEW YORK   NEW DELHI   SYDNEY

BLOOMSBURY EDUCATION
Bloomsbury Publishing Plc
50 Bedford Square, London, WC1B 3DP, UK
29 Earlsfort Terrace, Dublin 2, Ireland

BLOOMSBURY, BLOOMSBURY EDUCATION and the Diana logo are trademarks of
Bloomsbury Publishing Plc

First published in Great Britain, 2020 by Bloomsbury Publishing Plc
Text copyright © Andrew Jennings, 2020

Ninja illustrations copyright © Andrew Jennings, 2020
Illustrations copyright © Ilias Arahovitis, 2020

Andrew Jennings has asserted his right under the Copyright, Designs and Patents Act, 1988,
to be identified as Author of this work

Bloomsbury Publishing Plc does not have any control over, or responsibility for, any third-party
websites referred to or in this book. All internet addresses given in this book were correct
at the time of going to press. The author and publisher regret any inconvenience caused if
addresses have changed or sites have ceased to exist, but can accept no responsibility for any
such changes

All rights reserved. No part of this publication may be reproduced or transmitted in any
form or by any means, electronic or mechanical, including photocopying, recording, or any
information storage or retrieval system, without prior permission in writing from
the publishers

A catalogue record for this book is available from the British Library

ISBN: PB: 978-1-4729-8504-0; ePDF: 978-1-4729-8506-4

6 8 10 9 7 5

Text design by Marcus Duck Design

Printed and bound in India by Manipal Technologies Limited

To find out more about our authors and books visit www.bloomsbury.com
and sign up for our newsletters

Acknowledgements

Without Paul Watson's supportive conversations and the inspiring words within them,
Vocabulary Ninja and Comprehension Ninja would undoubtedly never have become a reality.
I'm proud to call him a friend and even prouder that he could be a part of the
Comprehension Ninja series.

NTRODUCTION

Reading comprehension is all about understanding what you are reading – and being able to show that you understand. This Comprehension Ninja workbook will help your child master the foundations of reading comprehension by focusing on three key aspects:

- **Skimming** and **scanning** a whole text to locate information efficiently.
- **Retrieving** the correct information from the text in eight different ways.
- **Vocabulary** awareness and the **effect of word choices.**

This book contains seven curriculum-linked texts, each followed by a set of questions to check whether your child has understood the text. There are eight question types to develop your child's comprehension skills:

For texts 1 - 4, the activity pages feature one question type per page so your child can focus on building up their comprehension skills one at a time, while texts 5 - 7 look a bit more like a test, with two pages of mixed questions.
This book includes the following topics: Mahatma Gandhi, Stone Age life, renewable energy, Pompeii, chocolate, the water cycle and the history of the charts.

HOW TO USE THIS WORKBOOK
STEP 1 – READ THE TEXT CAREFULLY

Encourage your child to read the whole text carefully before they start trying to answer the questions. You can help them with any words or phrases they don't know. As an extra activity, you could ask your child to read the text aloud to you.

STEP 2 – PICK OUT KEY WORDS AND INFORMATION

Picking out key words and headings will help your child to quickly locate the information they need to answer the questions. Encourage your child to underline key information as they read the text, such as:

- **Nouns** – names of people, places and objects.
- **Time** – dates and periods of time.
- **Numbers** – amounts, statistics, percentages and figures.
- **Vocabulary** – important topic vocabulary or words they are unsure of. They could look these up online or in a dictionary to find out what they mean.

Your child should also look out for titles and headings, which will help them understand the structure of the text.

STEP 3 – IDENTIFY KEY WORDS IN THE QUESTIONS

Encourage your child to identify key words in the questions so they know what they're looking for to find the answer. For example, in a text about the seaside:

   Question: What might you find in a rock pool?

   Key words: rock pool

'Rock pool' is the clue needed to answer the question.

STEP 4 – SKIM AND SCAN THE TEXT

Once your child has identified the key words in the question, they can try to remember where in the text the answer can be found. This might be as simple as remembering whether it was at the beginning, middle or end of the text, or thinking about which section the key information was in.

Your child can then **skim read** the whole text to find the section they need. When they've found it, they should **scan** the section to find the relevant sentences. They then read those sentences carefully to find the answer.

Invite your child to work through all the questions and give them lots of encouragement along the way. The answers can be found at the back of the book.

3

1 THE LIFE OF MAHATMA GANDHI

Mahatma Gandhi was an extraordinary activist and champion for justice. This is the story of how he changed the world.

Gandhi was born on 2 October, 1869, in Porbandar, India. His birth name was Mohandas Gandhi. He lived in England between the ages of 19 and 22, and became a lawyer.

When he returned home, Gandhi was shocked by the cruel way the British rulers and other white people treated Indian, Chinese and black people. He wanted to work to stop this injustice, but he saw the damage that riots could do.

Instead, Gandhi developed his own method of peaceful protest. He encouraged people to show the power of a cause by marching, sitting peacefully in the street or refusing to work. If one or two people did these actions, they wouldn't have been noticed – but Gandhi convinced thousands of people to join him.

Gandhi worked to change many laws, and made many people angry. He convinced people across India to wear Indian rather than British cloth, and was arrested for this. He later fought against tax on salt by marching 241 miles to the sea to make his own. This was known as the Salt March. Thousands of Indians joined him, and the law was changed. Gandhi also succeeded in changing laws that allowed people to mistreat the poorest members of Indian communities.

By changing these laws, Gandhi showed Indian people that they could stand up for their rights. His work led up to a protest against British rule in India – but he was arrested again.

Gandhi's treatment made Indian people more passionate for change. When he was released, Gandhi showed he had not given up on the cause. After World War II, he led vast peaceful protests against British rule. Finally, independence was granted.

Many people were still angry about the system Gandhi supported, though. After all his work, he was shot while attending a prayer meeting in 1948.

Gandhi came to be called 'Mahatma', meaning 'great soul', all over the world. He is also called 'Bapu', which means 'father'. Gandhi's great soul showed how to change the world with peaceful actions. He became the father of justice and independence.

1 THE LIFE OF MAHATMA GANDHI

FILL IN THE GAP

Read the sentences and choose the correct word or words to fill in the gap. Look back at *The life of Mahatma Gandhi* to find the correct answer.

Mahatma Gandhi was an extraordinary activist and _____ for justice.

Instead, Gandhi developed his own method of peaceful _____.

Gandhi came to be called _____, meaning 'great soul', all over the world.

He became the _____ of justice and independence.

Look back at paragraphs 3 and 4 in *The life of Mahatma Gandhi* to find the correct answer.

When he returned home, Gandhi was shocked by the cruel way the _____ and other white people treated Indian, Chinese and black people.

He wanted to work to stop this _____, but he saw the damage that riots could do.

He encouraged people to show the power of a cause by marching, sitting peacefully in the street or _____ to work.

If one or two people did these actions, they wouldn't have been noticed – but Gandhi convinced _____ of people to join him.

Look back at paragraph 5 in *The life of Mahatma Gandhi* to find the correct answer.

Gandhi worked to change many laws, and made many people _____.

This was known as the _____.

He later fought against tax on salt by marching _____ miles to the sea to make his own.

_____ of Indians joined him, and the law was changed.

1 THE LIFE OF MAHATMA GANDHI

MATCHING

Draw a line with a ruler to match the information. One has already been done for you.

1948	•	•	Gandhi born
thousands	•	•	Gandhi shot
241 miles	•	•	length of the Salt March
1869	•	•	people on the Salt March

Draw a line with a ruler to match the information.

worked in England as	•	•	marching and sitting peacefully
peaceful protest	•	•	Salt March
refused to wear	•	•	lawyer
famous protest	•	•	British cloth

Draw a line with a ruler to match the information.

champion for	•	•	Bapu
born in	•	•	justice
known as	•	•	great soul
Mahatma means	•	•	Porbandar

1 THE LIFE OF MAHATMA GANDHI
◉ MULTIPLE CHOICE

Circle the correct answer to the following questions.

In which year was Gandhi born?

| 1989 | 1896 | 1986 | 1869 |

How many people joined Gandhi on the Salt March?

| tens | hundreds | thousands | millions |

How many miles did Gandhi walk on the Salt March?

| 241 | 421 | 124 | 242 |

What does Mahatma mean?

| great man | great manager | great Indian | great soul |

Which job did Gandhi do in England?

| teacher | priest | lawyer | doctor |

What was Gandhi's birth name?

| Hatma Gandhi | Mohandas Gandhi | Mohat Gandhi | Mo Gandhi |

What does 'Bapu' mean?

| mother | protester | soul | father |

What was Gandhi the father of?

| justice and independence | peace and justice | freedom | independence and freedom |

1 THE LIFE OF MAHATMA GANDHI

👍 TRUE OR FALSE

Read the sentences. Put a tick in the correct box to show which sentences are *true* and which are *false*.

Mahatma Gandhi was born in London.	True ☐	False ☐
Mahatma Gandhi died in 1869.	True ☐	False ☐
His birth name was Mohandas.	True ☐	False ☐
The British rulers were cruel to Indian, Chinese and black people.	True ☐	False ☐
Gandhi was a lawyer.	True ☐	False ☐
Gandhi marched 280 miles.	True ☐	False ☐
Gandhi marched to the sea to make his own salt.	True ☐	False ☐
Millions of Indians joined him on the Salt March.	True ☐	False ☐
Gandhi got the law changed.	True ☐	False ☐
Gandhi died in his sleep.	True ☐	False ☐
Gandhi is known as Bapu, which means 'father'.	True ☐	False ☐
Gandhi was arrested a number of times.	True ☐	False ☐
Gandhi believed in peaceful protests.	True ☐	False ☐
During peaceful protests, Gandhi would sit in the street.	True ☐	False ☐
He lived in England between the ages of 15 and 32.	True ☐	False ☐

2 STONE AGE LIFE

The Stone Age was the time when humans used stone tools, before they worked with metal. It started around 3.4 million years ago. It ended between 8,000 and 4,500 years ago, when people started using copper.

In the Stone Age, people had two concerns: finding food and protecting themselves. Staying safe and alive was a full-time job.

Stone tools helped people to fight, explore their surroundings and, most importantly, to hunt animals and make fire. At the start of the Stone Age, humans only had caves for shelter. They stayed warm by wearing animal skins and with fires. Both of these relied on stone tools. The tools were not always rough and basic, though.

Stone was used with leather, bone and wood. Stone Age needles were made out of animal bones, meaning better clothes could be made. Stone blades were also fixed to wooden poles to make spears. These allowed people to hunt and kill animals with less danger to themselves.

Eating meat gave early humans the strength and energy to grow bigger and better than their ancestors. Being able to cook meat on a fire meant it was easier to digest – which gave them even more energy. This meant humans also grew cleverer.

Inside their caves, humans left their mark by painting stories onto the walls. Scenes of caveman hunting animals, and of natural landmarks, have been found across the globe and studied by historians. This is how we know about Stone Age life, millions of years later. People have suggested that the paintings were used to teach others, not just as decorations. They may have been used as instructions and maps.

By the end of the Stone Age, people had developed much more impressive ways of working. People grew plants and kept animals on purpose, making the first farms. They also began to create simple houses with protective roofs, which meant they could move away from the caves. They could live in communities, close to water, and on better land to grow plants on.

Finding food and protection became easier and easier. Humans could start to focus on developing as intelligent people.

2 STONE AGE LIFE

✏ FILL IN THE GAP

**Read the sentences and choose the correct word or words to fill in the gap.
Look back at paragraph 1 in *Stone Age life* to find the correct answer.**

The _____ was the time when humans used stone tools, before they worked with metal.

It started around _____ years ago.

It ended between 8,000 and 4,500 years ago, when people started using _____.

Look back at paragraph 3 in *Stone Age life* to find the correct answer.

Stone tools helped people to fight, explore their surroundings and, most importantly, to _____ animals and make fire.

At the start of the Stone Age, humans only had _____ for shelter.

The tools were not always _____ and basic, though.

Look back at paragraph 7 in *Stone Age life* to find the correct answer.

They also began to create simple houses with _____ roofs, which meant they could move away from the caves.

By the end of the Stone Age, people had developed much more _____ ways of working.

People grew plants and kept _____ on purpose, making the first farms.

They could live in _____, close to water, and on better land to grow plants on.

2 STONE AGE LIFE

MATCHING

Draw a line with a ruler to match the information. One has already been done for you.

full-time job	—	animal bones
needles made from		finding food and protecting themselves
their only shelter		staying safe
two concerns		caves

(full-time job is connected to staying safe)

Draw a line with a ruler to match the information.

important part of the Stone Age		cleverer
fire		fire
clothes made from		keep warm
humans grew		animal fur

Draw a line with a ruler to match the information.

painted walls		3.4 million years ago
Stone Age began		instructions and maps
paintings may have been		inside caves
humans used stone		before metal

2 STONE AGE LIFE

◎ MULTIPLE CHOICE

Circle the correct answer to the following questions.

What type of needle was used to make clothes?

| tools | stone | bone | wood |

What can still be found inside Stone Age caves today?

| clothing | tools | painted walls | fire |

When did the Stone Age begin?

| 1.4 million years ago | 2.4 million years ago | 3.4 million years ago | 4.4 million years ago |

What was an important part of Stone Age life?

| fire | jogging | copper | socialising |

What did later Stone Age humans create?

| protective roofs | heating | water systems | spears and arrows |

How did Stone Age people stay warm?

| by wearing animal skins | by buying blankets | by running around | by exploring their surroundings |

What were the two main concerns for Stone Age people?

| food and protection | killing animals and relaxing | relaxing and finding water | making fires and painting |

What did humans focus on at the end of the Stone Age?

| sleeping | cooking meat | becoming intelligent | finding food |

14

2 STONE AGE LIFE

👍 TRUE OR FALSE

Read the sentences. Put a tick in the correct box to show which sentences are *true* and which are *false*.

The Stone Age began 3.4 million years ago.	True ☐	False ☐
Humans invented stone tools during the Bronze Age.	True ☐	False ☐
Staying safe and alive was a part-time job.	True ☐	False ☐
Stone Age humans used stone tools to hunt.	True ☐	False ☐
Stone Age humans stayed warm by wearing animal skins.	True ☐	False ☐
Humans lived in houses at the start of the Stone Age.	True ☐	False ☐
Stone Age humans painted cave walls to share stories.	True ☐	False ☐
Stone Age humans lived in caves.	True ☐	False ☐
The two main concerns were food and copper.	True ☐	False ☐
Stone Age humans used plants and grass for clothes.	True ☐	False ☐
Bones were crafted into needles.	True ☐	False ☐
Fire allowed humans to cook meat.	True ☐	False ☐
The Stone Age ended when people started using copper.	True ☐	False ☐
In the Stone Age, people had five concerns.	True ☐	False ☐
By the end of the Stone Age, some people had farms.	True ☐	False ☐
Finding food became easier and easier.	True ☐	False ☐

2 STONE AGE LIFE

👀 FIND AND COPY

These questions are about *Stone Age life*.

Look at paragraph 2. Find and copy a word that suggests that Stone Age humans had two things to worry or be anxious about.

_____

Look at the paragraph beginning 'By the end of the Stone Age…' and copy a word that suggests that Stone Age humans lived in groups.

_____

Look at the paragraph beginning 'By the end of the Stone Age…' and copy a word that describes the roofs that Stone Age people created.

_____

Look at the final paragraph. Find and copy a word that describes what type of people humans focused on becoming.

_____

2 STONE AGE LIFE

UNDERLINE OR HIGHLIGHT

Read the paragraphs below and then follow the instructions.

> Eating meat gave early humans the strength and energy to grow bigger and better than their ancestors. Being able to cook meat on a fire meant it was easier to digest – which gave them even more energy. This meant humans also grew cleverer.
>
> Inside their caves, humans left their mark by painting stories onto the walls. Scenes of caveman hunting animals, and of natural landmarks, have been found across the globe and studied by historians. This is how we know about Stone Age life, millions of years later. People have suggested that the paintings were used to teach others, not just as decorations. They may have been used as instructions and maps.

Underline or highlight a word that means people we are descended from.

Underline or highlight a word that is a type of job where people study the past.

Underline or highlight a word that means to track and kill animals for food.

Underline or highlight a word that means to break down food.

Underline or highlight another word for 'Earth' or 'sphere'.

3 RENEWABLE ENERGY SOURCES

Humans have always needed sources of energy. They have burned coal, oil and natural gas to create heat and light. All of these natural resources are taken from the Earth. None of them can be put back. This is what the term 'non-renewable' means.

In recent decades, humans have understood that these non-renewable resources are running out. They have also learned that burning them hurts the environment. It is becoming more and more important to use renewable energy sources.

The sun, water, the wind, the Earth, plants and animals can all be renewable energy sources.

Solar power is energy from the Sun. In the past, people have used it directly, to do things such as dry clothes. Now we have ways of turning the sunlight into electrical energy using solar cells. These small cells are put together to create larger solar panels. You may have seen solar panels on the roofs of some buildings.

Hydroelectric energy is energy from flowing water. In the past, water has been used to turn watermill wheels. Hydroelectric energy is created in a similar way. The water turns a turbine, and its spinning energy can then be turned into electricity.

Wind power also turns turbines that make electricity. Wind farms are made up of tall windmills. They can often be found near the coast or on hills, where the wind is strongest. Wind farms allow humans to collect energy on a large scale, but some people don't like the way they change the landscape.

Biomass fuel is made of waste from growing plants or raising animals. It can even be made from human waste. The waste can create heat energy when it rots, or chemicals can be taken from it. The chemicals can be used to make fuel. Some cars can run on biomass fuel instead of petrol or diesel.

Geothermal energy is the heat that the Earth produces naturally. There are places in the world where the Earth's crust is quite thin. There, the lava below is close enough that we can use its heat energy. It is difficult to use a lot of geothermal heat because the locations are rare.

3 RENEWABLE ENERGY SOURCES

✏ FILL IN THE GAP

Read the sentences and choose the correct word or words to fill in the gap. Look back at the paragraph about 'Solar power' in *Renewable energy sources* to find the correct answer.

Solar power is _____ from the Sun.

In the past, people have used it directly, to do things such as _____.

Now we have ways of turning the sunlight into _____ energy using solar cells.

These small cells are put together to create larger _____.

You may have seen solar panels on the _____ of some buildings.

Look back at the paragraph about 'Biomass fuel' in *Renewable energy sources* to find the correct answer.

Biomass fuel is made of _____ from growing plants or raising animals.

It can even be made from _____ waste.

The waste can create heat energy when it _____, or chemicals can be taken from it.

The chemicals can be used to make fuel. Some _____ can run on biomass fuel.

Look back at the paragraph about 'Wind power' in *Renewable energy sources* to find the correct answer.

Wind power also turns _____ that make electricity.

Wind farms are made up of _____ windmills.

They can often be found near the _____ or on hills, where the wind is strongest.

Wind farms allow humans to collect energy on a large scale, but some people don't like the way they _____ the landscape.

3 RENEWABLE ENERGY SOURCES

MATCHING

Draw a line with a ruler to match the information. One has already been done for you.

solar	•——————•	waste	
hydroelectric	• •	sun	
biomass	• •	water	
geothermal	• •	Earth's heat	

Draw a line with a ruler to match the information.

watermills	• •	biomass	
windmills	• •	hydroelectric	
solar panels	• •	wind	
plants or animals	• •	solar	

Draw a line with a ruler to match the information.

geothermal	• •	panels	
hydroelectric	• •	used in some cars	
solar	• •	uses water	
biomass	• •	lava emits heat	

3 RENEWABLE ENERGY SOURCES
LABEL

Label the information with the correct type of renewable energy.

Uses small cells to create larger panels	
Uses the heat that the Earth creates	
Generated from flowing water	
Created when waste rots	
Uses wind turbines to create electricity	
Produced from plants and animals	

Label the information with the correct type of renewable energy.

Watermills were used in the past to create	
Collects sunlight and turns it to electricity	
Much like hydroelectric, it uses nature to create energy through movement	
Uses lava's heat energy	
Used to dry clothes	

Draw the statement in the boxes. Add your own labels to your drawing.

solar	hydroelectric
biomass	geothermal

3 RENEWABLE ENERGY SOURCES

123 SEQUENCING

Look at the sentence below. Write the numbers 1 to 4 to show the order the words occur in the sentence.

Wind farms allow humans to collect energy on a large scale, but some people don't like the way they change the landscape.

collect	scale	farms	people

Look at paragraphs 1 and 2 in *Renewable energy sources*. Number the statements from 1 to 5 to show the order they occur in the text.

They have also learned that burning them hurts the environment. ☐

Humans have always needed sources of energy. ☐

It is becoming more and more important to use renewable energy sources. ☐

This is what the term 'non-renewable' means. ☐

All of these natural resources are taken from the Earth. ☐

Look at *Renewable energy sources*. Number the statements from 1 to 5 to show the order they occur in the text. Look at the first line of each paragraph to help you.

Hydroelectric energy is energy from flowing water. ☐

Wind power also turns turbines that make electricity. ☐

Geothermal energy is the heat that the Earth produces naturally. ☐

Solar power is energy from the Sun. ☐

Biomass fuel is made of waste from growing plants or raising animals. ☐

3 RENEWABLE ENERGY SOURCES

FIND AND COPY

These questions are about *Renewable energy sources*.

Look at paragraph 2. Find and copy a word that suggests that the energy source isn't used up.

_____

Look at the 'Solar power' section. Find and copy a word that tells us about the size of the solar cells.

_____

Look at the 'Hydroelectric energy' section. Find and copy a word that suggests that water is continuously moving.

_____

Look at the 'Geothermal energy' section. Find and copy a word that suggests that using geothermal energy is not easy.

_____

3 RENEWABLE ENERGY SOURCES

UNDERLINE OR HIGHLIGHT

Read the paragraphs below and then follow the instructions.

> Humans have always needed sources of energy. They have burned coal, oil and natural gas to create heat and light. All of these natural resources are taken from the Earth. None of them can be put back. This is what the term 'non-renewable' means.
>
> In recent decades, humans have understood that these non-renewable resources are running out. They have also learned that burning them hurts the environment. It is becoming more and more important to use renewable energy sources.

Underline or highlight a word that means that it comes from nature.

Underline or highlight a word that means the natural world around us.

Underline or highlight a word that means warmth.

Underline or highlight a phrase that means you will soon have no more of something.

Underline or highlight a word that means something is always available.

4 POMPEII

Pompeii was an ordinary city in the Roman Empire. It had theatres, temples, bathhouses, markets and pubs. It was in a beautiful location, too, close to the bay of Naples and the green slopes of the mountain Vesuvius.

In August of the year 79 CE, there had been some earth tremors in Pompeii, but the people weren't worried. The morning of 24 August was just like any other. Then, at around midday, a huge cloud of burning-hot gas and rocks filled the sky. Many people ran for the coast. Some went to fetch their belongings. Some hid indoors until the rocks stopped falling.

Those who survived may have felt relief, but the most powerful eruption came the next day. Volcanic ash and a flow of magma covered the city, killing everyone and everything still there. No one in Pompeii knew that they lived at the foot of an active volcano until it was too late.

For nearly 1,500 years, the city of Pompeii was lost to the sands of time – or, more accurately, to the ash of the volcano! Some of Pompeii's wall paintings were seen in 1592, but they were covered again. It wasn't until 1748 that archaeologists worked to unearth the lost city. People had to dig five metres to uncover the streets of Pompeii.

Workers discovered that the last moments of the city had been frozen in time. The heat from the volcano, and the way rain mixed with the ash, had created a protective shell. Even the bodies of the people of Pompeii had been encrusted in the ash. Over time, the bodies decayed, leaving just the empty shells. Soon, people realised that they could pour plaster into the shells to see how people in Pompeii had looked – and how they were behaving when they died.

Because of this, the disaster provided us with a clear model of life during Roman times. We are able to explore the buildings where people lived, the art they created and how they traded. In a way, the deaths of Pompeii's people were able to bring Roman times to life for the modern world.

4 POMPEII
LABEL

Label the information with the correct object or name.

People who had to dig to uncover the streets of Pompeii	
Name of the mountain beside Pompeii	
Mount Vesuvius was a	
A huge cloud of	
The most powerful	
A flow of	

Label the information with the correct information.

The disaster provides a clear model of life in	
Bodies of Pompeii were encrusted in	
The lost city of Pompeii was unearthed in	
Mount Vesuvius erupted on	
Empty shells remain after	
Pompeii was an ordinary city in	

Draw the statement in the boxes. Add your own labels to your drawing.

archaeologists discovering the streets	Mount Vesuvius
people of Pompeii	burning-hot gas and rocks filling the sky

28

4 POMPEII

123 SEQUENCING

Look at the sentence below. Write the numbers 1 to 4 to show the order the words occur in the sentence.

Then, at around midday, a huge cloud of burning-hot gas and rocks filled the sky.

sky	burning-hot	rocks	midday

Look at paragraph 2 in *Pompeii*. Number the statements from 1 to 5 to show the order they occur in the text.

Many people ran for the coast.

The morning of 24 August was just like any other.

Some went to fetch their belongings.

Then, at around midday, a huge cloud of burning-hot gas and rocks filled the sky.

In August of the year 79 CE, there had been some earth tremors in Pompeii, but the people weren't worried.

Look at *Pompeii*. Number the statements from 1 to 5 to show the order they occur in the text. Look at the first line of each paragraph to help you.

For nearly 1,500 years, the city of Pompeii was lost to the sands of time – or, more accurately, to the ash of the volcano!

Because of this, the disaster provided us with a clear model of life during Roman times.

Those who survived may have felt relief, but the most powerful eruption came the next day.

Pompeii was an ordinary city in the Roman Empire.

Workers discovered that the last moments of the city had been frozen in time.

4 POMPEII
◎ MULTIPLE CHOICE

Circle the correct answer to the following questions.

Mount Vesuvius erupted on which date?

| 24 August | 24 March | 24 April | 24 September |

When were Pompeii's wall paintings seen?

| 1792 | 1569 | 1592 | 1952 |

When was Pompeii unearthed by archaeologists?

| 1763 | 1748 | 1736 | 1784 |

Which of the following filled the air after the most powerful eruption?

| sunshine | rain | ash | rocks |

What flowed through the city?

| trade | people | magma | volcanoes |

What mixed with the ash to create a protective shell?

| rain | stones | people | magma |

Pompeii gives an insight into what life was like in…

| the Stone Age | Roman times | modern England | Spain |

30

4 POMPEII

👎 TRUE OR FALSE

Read the sentences. Put a tick in the correct box to show which sentences are *true* and which are *false*.

Statement	True	False
Pompeii is a volcano.	☐	☐
Mount Vesuvius is a town that was destroyed.	☐	☐
Disaster struck on 24 August 79 CE.	☐	☐
Nobody was injured in the disaster.	☐	☐
No one was ready for the volcanic eruption.	☐	☐
The people of Pompeii knew they were living next to a volcano.	☐	☐
After the eruption, gas and rocks filled the sky.	☐	☐
It took weeks for the city to be buried in rock and ash.	☐	☐
Magma flowed in the city.	☐	☐
Pompeii was unearthed again in 1748.	☐	☐
Scientists had to dig down six metres to find the city of Pompeii.	☐	☐
The ash and lava froze the city in time.	☐	☐
Evidence of art, buildings and trading can be found in the remains.	☐	☐
Bodies decayed over time, but empty shells remained.	☐	☐
Pompeii's people were able to bring Roman times to life for the modern world.	☐	☐

4 POMPEII

FIND AND COPY

These questions are about *Pompeii*.

Look at paragraph 1. Find and copy a word that suggests that Pompeii was just like any other Roman city.

_____

Look at paragraph 3. Find and copy a word that tells us what the people who survived may have felt.

_____

Look at paragraph 4. Find and copy a word that suggests that archaeologists dug Pompeii out of the ground.

_____

Look at paragraph 5. Find and copy a word that suggests that bodies were covered in a hard surface of ash.

_____

 **4** POMPEII

UNDERLINE OR HIGHLIGHT

Read the paragraphs below and then follow the instructions.

> Workers discovered that the last moments of the city had been frozen in time. The heat from the volcano, and the way rain mixed with the ash, had created a protective shell. Even the bodies of the people of Pompeii had been encrusted in the ash. Over time, the bodies decayed, leaving just the empty shells. Soon, people realised that they could pour plaster into the shells to see how people in Pompeii had looked – and how they were behaving when they died.
>
> Because of this, the disaster provided us with a clear model of life during Roman times. We are able to explore the buildings where people lived, the art they created and how they traded. In a way, the deaths of Pompeii's people were able to bring Roman times to life for the modern world.

Underline or highlight a word that means a sudden accident or natural catastrophe.

Underline or highlight a word that means that something has broken down after death.

Underline or highlight a word that means to stop something from being harmed.

Underline or highlight a word that means a smooth paste that becomes hard when it dries.

Underline or highlight a word that means a hard outer case.

5 CHOCOLATE

The chocolate you eat has had a long journey before it gets to you – in distance and in time!

Chocolate is made from cocoa beans, which grow in tropical regions. 70% of the world's cocoa beans comes from four West African countries: Ivory Coast, Ghana, Nigeria and Cameroon. Lots also come from Indonesia, and from Central America – which is the place where the history of chocolate began.

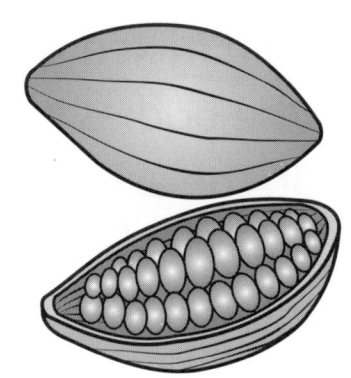

Evidence of chocolate production has been found from almost 4,000 years ago. The Olmec people may have been the first to work with it then. Many ancient peoples used chocolate, including the Maya and the Aztecs. It was normally made into thick, bitter drinks. There was no sugar, so it was flavoured with other things – often, chilli! Chocolate was precious enough to be used like money. It was also used in religious rituals.

When Europeans arrived in Central America, they loved the taste of chocolate. They took cocoa beans back to Europe with them. People in Europe experimented with heating the chocolate drink, and adding cream and sugar. They found a way to make solid bars of this creamy, sweet chocolate, creating the chocolate we know today.

Making chocolate is a complicated process.

1. First, cocoa pods are picked from trees. The beans inside are cleaned and dried.
2. Next, the dry beans are roasted to bring out their flavour. In chocolate factories, they are roasted on huge trays. Their shells become brittle as they cool, making them easy to remove.
3. The broken-up bits of roasted cocoa bean are called nibs. The nibs are ground to create a thick paste.
4. The paste is squashed by powerful machines. Cocoa butter is squeezed out, leaving a block of cocoa powder. We can use the cocoa powder in cooking and hot chocolate.
5. Bars of sweet chocolate are made by mixing cocoa powder and cocoa butter carefully and adding sugar. Other ingredients, like milk and vanilla, can be added, too.

Chocolate can be dark, milk or white, depending on the mix of bitter cocoa powder and sweet cocoa butter. They can all be delicious!

⏵ FILL IN THE GAP

Look back at *Chocolate*. Skim to find the correct area or paragraph of the text. Then scan to locate the correct sentence. Fill in the gap with the missing word.

When _____ arrived in Central America, they loved the taste of chocolate.

The broken-up bits of _____ cocoa bean are called nibs.

....

⏵ MATCHING

Draw a line with a ruler to match the information. One has already been done for you.

West African countries		tropical regions
cocoa beans grow		experimented with heating chocolate
people in Europe		70% of the world's cocoa beans

....

⏵ LABEL

Label the information with the correct step of the chocolate-making process.

Beans are cleaned	
Vanilla may be added	
Dry beans are roasted	
Nibs ground to a paste	
Cocoa butter is squeezed out	

....

⏵ TRUE OR FALSE

Read the sentences. Put a tick in the correct box to show which sentences are *true* and which are *false*.

Cocoa beans grow all over the world.   True ☐   False ☐

The Maya people used chocolate.   True ☐   False ☐

Chocolate can be dark, milk or white.   True ☐   False ☐

◎ MULTIPLE CHOICE

Circle the correct answer to the following question.

In which region does 70% of the world's cocoa grow?

| East Africa | West Africa | North Africa | South Africa |

123 SEQUENCING

Look at *Chocolate*. Number the statements from 1 to 3 to show the order they occur in the text.

They found a way to make solid bars of this creamy, sweet chocolate, creating the chocolate we know today.	
Lots also come from Indonesia, and from Central America – which is the place where the history of chocolate began.	
The broken-up bits of roasted cocoa bean are called nibs.	

👀 FIND AND COPY

Read the sentences below. Find and copy a word that suggests that the nibs are crushed.

The broken-up bits of roasted cocoa bean are called nibs. The nibs are ground to create a thick paste.

_____

🔦 UNDERLINE OR HIGHLIGHT

Read the following sentence. Underline or highlight a word that means raise the temperature of something.

People in Europe experimented with heating the chocolate drink, and adding cream and sugar.

6 THE WATER CYCLE

Water is vital to all life on Earth. The planet couldn't even have developed life without it. Around 70% of the Earth is covered in water. The water doesn't stay still, though: it is constantly moving and changing state.

What is the water cycle?

The water cycle is the way water moves around the Earth. Water can change state, which means it can be a liquid, a solid (which we know as ice) or a gas (which we know as steam or water vapour). The water cycle is possible because these changes of state are reversible. A drop of water can freeze, melt, boil, cool and freeze again an unlimited number of times.

Water's changes of state allow it to travel from the Earth's surface into the sky, around the world and back to the surface again. This water cycle happens constantly, everywhere.

Evaporation

Evaporation happens when a liquid is heated. It is the change of state from a liquid to a gas. In the water cycle, it happens when the sun shines down on the ocean, a lake, a river, or any other source of water. The sun heats the water, and the warm water vapour rises upwards.

Condensation

Condensation happens when a gas is cooled. It is the change of state from a gas to a liquid. Water vapour cools as it rises higher. It condenses slightly to form clouds. As more water vapour cools, the clouds become bigger and heavier. The water droplets merge together, and form larger drops. When the cloud is heavy with drops, they fall as rain.

Precipitation

Precipitation is the falling of water from the sky back to Earth. This is the part of the water cycle that we can see most clearly. Precipitation can be rain, hail or snow. Snow and hail are frozen water. Hail shows another change of state: the change from a liquid to a solid.

The rain that doesn't land directly in the ocean usually finds its way there through streams and rivers. Wherever the water is, though, the cycle will soon start again!

FILL IN THE GAP

Look back at *The water cycle*. Skim to find the correct area or paragraph of the text. Then scan to locate the correct sentence. Fill in the gap with the missing word.

Around _____ of the Earth is covered in water.

As more water vapour cools, the _____ become bigger and heavier.

MATCHING

Draw a line with a ruler to match the information. One has already been done for you.

water vapour cools	•	•	evaporation
water falls to earth	•	•	precipitation
water is heated and becomes a gas	•	•	condensation

(water vapour cools — condensation line already drawn)

LABEL

Label the information with the correct stage of the water cycle.

Water rises up into the atmosphere	
Rain, hail or even snow falls	
Water vapour begins to form clouds	
Rain runs into rivers and streams	
Water vapour cools as it gets higher	

TRUE OR FALSE

Read the sentences. Put a tick in the correct box to show which sentences are *true* and which are *false*.

80% of the Earth is covered in water.   True ☐   False ☐

The Earth's water stays in the same place.   True ☐   False ☐

When liquid is heated, it evaporates.   True ☐   False ☐

◎ MULTIPLE CHOICE

Circle the correct answer to the following question.

In which stage of the water cycle might water fall to Earth as hail?

| condensation | freezing | evaporation | precipitation |

123 SEQUENCING

Look at *The water cycle*. Number the statements from 1 to 3 to show the order they occur in the text.

In the water cycle, it happens when the sun shines down on the ocean, a lake, a river, or any other source of water.	
The water cycle is the way water moves around the Earth.	
This is the part of the water cycle that we can see most clearly.	

👓 FIND AND COPY

Read the sentence below. Find and copy a word that suggests that the water cycle is always happening.

The water doesn't stay still, though: it is constantly moving and changing state.

_____

◐ UNDERLINE OR HIGHLIGHT

Read the sentence below. Underline or highlight a word that means capable of changing back to an original state.

The water cycle is possible because these changes of state are reversible.

7 THE HISTORY OF THE CHARTS

Every musician dreams of having a best-selling song reach number one in the charts – but what are 'the charts', and how did we start using them?

The charts are rankings of the sales of 'singles'. They chart the success of individual songs.

In the United Kingdom, the first charting of music sales was done in 1952, by the editor of a magazine called the NME (the New Musical Express). Percy Dickins telephoned record shops and requested sales numbers for the records that had sold the most. Dickins then ordered the songs by popularity, and published this chart in his magazine. He had no way of knowing what his idea had begun!

In 1969, the BBC became involved. They wanted to create content that would be popular with younger people, and knew that music was a good way to do it. The BBC was able to request sales figures from far more shops, which made the chart more accurate. At the end of business each Saturday, around 6,000 shops sent in their receipts for the week. The receipts were counted over the weekend, and the chart was broadcast each Sunday evening, ranking the music bought from the 40th to the first most popular. For singers and bands, being the best-selling artist quickly became a goal.

As the way we listen to music changed, so did the way the data were collected. By 1980, shop records were kept digitally. This meant they could be transferred to create the BBC's charts without receipts having to be counted by hand.

In the 2000s, music purchases changed again, when downloading music became the most popular form of buying it. Downloaded music was first included in the charts in 2007. The bigger change came in 2014, when streamed music was also included. For the first time, songs did not have to be bought individually to count in the charts.

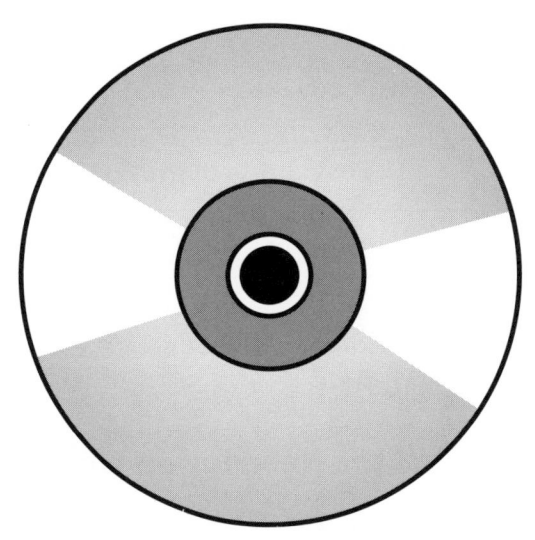

Critics have said that recognising free streaming reduces the value of music. The charts have never been meant to instruct the way people buy music, though. They simply chart it.

7 THE HISTORY OF THE CHARTS

✏️ FILL IN THE GAP

Look back at *The history of the charts*. Skim to find the correct area or paragraph of the text. Then scan to locate the correct sentence. Fill in the gap with the missing word.

In the United Kingdom, the first charting of music sales was done in 1952, by the _____ of a magazine called the NME.

The BBC was able to request sales figures from far more shops, which made the chart more _____.

....

🎧 MATCHING

Draw a line with a ruler to match the information. One has already been done for you.

Downloads became part of the chart •	•	1952
First charts of music sales •	•	1969
The BBC became involved •	•	2007

....

✏️ LABEL

Label the description with the correct information.

NME means	
Editor of NME	
BBC wanted to be popular with	
Day of the week when the BBC collected sales figures	
Number of shops that sent in their receipts	

....

🎧 TRUE OR FALSE

Read the sentences. Put a tick in the correct box to show which sentences are *true* and which are *false*.

The BBC used to collect record sales from 6,000 stores.   True ☐   False ☐

Streaming music doesn't count towards the chart.   True ☐   False ☐

By 1970, shop records were kept digitally.   True ☐   False ☐

◎ MULTIPLE CHOICE

Circle the correct answer to the following question.

In which year was streamed music first included in the charts?

| 1969 | 1980 | 2007 | 2014 |

123 SEQUENCING

Look at *The history of the charts*. Number the statements from 1 to 3 to show the order they occur in the text.

The receipts were counted over the weekend, and the chart was broadcast each Sunday evening, ranking the music bought from the 40th to the first most popular.	
The charts are rankings of the sales of 'singles'.	
The charts have never been meant to instruct the way people buy music, though.	

👀 FIND AND COPY

Read the sentence below. Find and copy a word that tells us that something was liked by many people.

In the 2000s, music purchases changed again, when downloading music became the most popular form of buying it.

_____

◐ UNDERLINE OR HIGHLIGHT

Read the sentence below. Underline or highlight a word that means transmitted over a computer network.

The bigger change came in 2014, when streamed music was also included.

7 THE HISTORY OF THE CHARTS

45

1. THE LIFE OF MAHATMA GANDHI

FILL IN THE GAP

1. champion
2. protest
3. 'Mahatma'
4. father
5. British rulers
6. injustice
7. refusing
8. thousands
9. angry
10. Salt March
11. 241
12. Thousands

MATCHING

1948	Gandhi shot
thousands	people on the Salt March
241 miles	length of the Salt March
1869	Gandhi born
worked in England as	lawyer
peaceful protest	marching and sitting peacefully
refused to wear	British cloth
famous protest	Salt March
champion for	justice
born in	Porbandar
known as	Bapu
Mahatma means	great soul

MULTIPLE CHOICE

1869
thousands
241
great soul
lawyer
Mohandas Gandhi
father
justice and independence

TRUE OR FALSE

1. False
2. False
3. True
4. True
5. True
6. False
7. True
8. False
9. True
10. False
11. True
12. True
13. True
14. True
15. False

2. STONE AGE LIFE

FILL IN THE GAP

1. Stone Age
2. 3.4 million
3. copper
4. hunt
5. caves
6. rough
7. protective
8. impressive
9. animals
10. communities

MATCHING

full-time job	staying safe
needles made from	animal bones
their only shelter	caves
two concerns	finding food and protecting themselves
important part of the Stone Age	fire
fire	keep warm
clothes made from	animal fur
humans grew	cleverer
painted walls	inside caves
Stone Age began	3.4 million years ago
paintings may have been	instructions and maps
humans used stone	before metal

MULTIPLE CHOICE

bone
painted walls
3.4 million years ago
fire
protective roofs
by wearing animal skins
food and protection
becoming intelligent

TRUE OR FALSE

1. True
2. False
3. False
4. True
5. True
6. False
7. True
8. True
9. False
10. False
11. True
12. True
13. False
14. True
15. True

FIND AND COPY

concerns
communities
protective
intelligent

UNDERLINE OR HIGHLIGHT

ancestors
historians
hunting
digest
globe

3. RENEWABLE ENERGY SOURCES
FILL IN THE GAP
1. energy
2. dry clothes
3. electrical
4. solar panels
5. roofs
6. waste
7. human
8. rots
9. cars
10. turbines
11. tall
12. coast
13. change

MATCHING

solar	sun
hydroelectric	water
biomass	waste
geothermal	Earth's heat

watermills	hydroelectric
windmills	wind
solar panels	solar
plants or animals	biomass

geothermal	lava emits heat
hydroelectric	uses water
solar	panels
biomass	used in some cars

LABEL
solar power
geothermal energy
hydroelectric energy
biomass fuel
wind power
biomass fuel
hydroelectric energy
solar power
wind power
geothermal energy
solar power

SEQUENCING
2, 3, 1, 4
4, 1, 5, 3, 2
2, 3, 5, 1, 4

FIND AND COPY
renewable
small
flowing
difficult

UNDERLINE OR HIGHLIGHT
natural
environment
heat
non-renewable
renewable

4. POMPEII
LABEL
archaeologists
Vesuvius
volcano
gas and rocks
eruption
magma
Roman times
ash
1748
24 August
the bodies decayed
the Roman Empire

SEQUENCING
4, 2, 3, 1
4, 2, 5, 3, 1
3, 5, 2, 1, 4

MULTIPLE CHOICE
24 August
1592
1748
ash
magma
rain
Roman times

TRUE OR FALSE
1. False
2. False
3. True
4. False
5. True
6. False
7. True
8. False
9. True
10. True
11. False
12. True
13. True
14. True
15. True

FIND AND COPY
ordinary
relief
unearth
encrusted

UNDERLINE OR HIGHLIGHT
disaster
decayed
protective
plaster
shell

5. CHOCOLATE
FILL IN THE GAP
Europeans
roasted

MATCHING

West African countries	70% of the world's cocoa beans
cocoa beans grow	tropical regions
people in Europe	experimented with heating chocolate

LABEL
1
5
2
3
4

TRUE OR FALSE
False
True
True

MULTIPLE CHOICE
West Africa

SEQUENCING
2, 1, 3

FIND AND COPY
ground

UNDERLINE OR HIGHLIGHT
heating

6. THE WATER CYCLE
FILL IN THE GAP
70%
clouds

MATCHING

water vapour cools	condensation
water falls to earth	precipitation
water is heated and becomes a gas	evaporation

LABEL
evaporation
precipitation
condensation
precipitation
condensation

TRUE OR FALSE
False
False
True

MULTIPLE CHOICE
precipitation

SEQUENCING
2, 1, 3

FIND AND COPY
constantly

UNDERLINE OR HIGHLIGHT
reversible

7. THE HISTORY OF THE CHARTS
FILL IN THE GAP
editor
accurate

MATCHING

Downloads became part of the chart	2007
First charts of music sales	1952
The BBC became involved	1969

LABEL
New Musical Express
Percy Dickins
younger people
Saturday
6,000

TRUE OR FALSE
True
False
False

MULTIPLE CHOICE
2014

SEQUENCING
2, 1, 3

FIND AND COPY
popular

UNDERLINE OR HIGHLIGHT
streamed